T0154402

BRIGHT BODY

OTHER BOOKS BY ALIKI BARNSTONE

POETRY

The Real Tin Flower

Windows in Providence

Madly in Love

Wild With It

Blue Earth

Dear God, Dear Dr. Heartbreak: New and Selected Poems

TRANSLATION

The Collected Poems of C.P. Cavafy: A New Translation

ANTHOLOGIES

A Book of Women Poets from Antiquity to Now
with Willis Barnstone

The Calvinist Roots of the Modern Era
with Michael Manson & Carol J. Singley

The Shambhala Anthology of Women's Spiritual Poetry
(paperback edition of *Voices of Light:*
Spiritual and Visionary Poems by Women Around the World from Ancient Sumeria to Now)

EDITION

Trilogy by H.D.
Introduction and Readers' Notes by Aliki Barnstone

Bright Body

Aliki Barnstone

White Pine Press / Buffalo, New York

WHITE PINE PRESS
P.O. Box 236
BUFFALO, NEW YORK 14201

Publication of this book was made possible, in part, by a grant from the National
Endowment of the Arts, which believes that a great nation deserves great art,
and with public funds from the New York State Council on the Arts, a State Agency.

ACKNOWLEDGMENTS

Grateful acknowledgement to the journals in which these poems have appeared or will
appear:

The Colorado Review: "Civil Disobedience, New Year's, 1980" as "Resistance to Civil
Government, New Year's, 1980,"
Court Green: "Yellow Letter,"
Cutbank: "Your Name is the Boat,"
The Drunken Boat: "Guess What?" "I Don't Grow Wings, I Drive my Car," "A Las Vegas Dust
Storm," "The Lights of Las Vegas," "You Wake in the Shaded Room," "On the Eastern
Seaboard with Diane DiPrima," "The Storm," "Emily Dickinson in Las Vegas," "In the
Optometrist's Waiting Room," "Elegy for a Lover of Horses," "You Hate Windchimes," "A
Body Politic," "Photo Op," "Take a Deep Breath," "Close to Death," When I Think of the
Hand," "Days of 2003," "A Field of War," "Freeway Love Poem,"
Georgia Review: "Ephemeral Ethereal," "Chatterbox,"
Hotel Amerika: "At 3 a.m.," "Idealism,"
New Letters: "You Pray to Rain Falling in the Desert," "Macho Wind,"
North American Review: "In the Night Box,"
Pleiades: "You Play with Yourself," "Catherine and Eva,"
Poetry International: "Invitation to a Poet,"
Acknowledgments continue on page 120

Cover painting: "Red Airplane" by Felicia van Bork. Used by permission of the artist.

First Edition.

ISBN: 978-1-935210-24-5

Printed and bound in the United States of America.

Library of Congress Control Number: 2010933055

For Zoë, whose name is life

CONTENTS

— Bright Body —

As they could not reach me, they had resolved to punish my body.

—Henry David Thoreau

LIFE

Life is a new sunrise
and the ending of life is an old sundown.
My name is said in hospitals and churches and songs.
ZOË ZOË ZOË ZOË...LIFE LIFE LIFE.
My words are newborn's breath.
My name brings happiness into peoples lives.
My name is not only on land but in the sea,
in the air, in the trees. The one thing I hate
to see is death. It makes me feel that my name
has been crossed out of the person's heart.
But indeed it has.

—Zoë Barnstone-Clark,
age eight and a half

You Pray to Rain Falling on the Desert

because it is a Sunday where the sky is blue nearly every day
and you might forget to be sad.

Because you don't sing with a choir, except the quiet
rain intoning on the backyard patio—
and the raindrops outside are not the human voices
you must listen to.

Because in March rains wake up desert flowers
and globe mallow blooms everywhere—burning bushes
in the Valley of Fire and vacant lots waiting for gas stations.
You will see their orange blossoms flaring through your windshield,
and no voice will say *I am.*

Because the rain will swell Lake Mead with our water for drinking
and bathtubs and gardens full of thirsty grass, roses, and oleander.
Because the fatal bacteria will die in treatment plants.
Because there are no mosquitoes here, no malaria.
Because the Children's Hospital is stocked with medicine.

Because the rain will wash away dust and misery
and channel toxins from spent bombs into the ground water.

Because your daughter wanted to walk instead of drive
and she spun in her orange dress, pointed her pink-sneakered foot,
and curtseyed in the driveway
because rain on the desert is a multitude of tender hands
applauding new life.

It is the eve of war
and you don't believe the broadcast on radio and on television:
I will rid you out of their bondage
and I will redeem you with a stretched out arm,
and with great judgments.

Because the rain keeps you inward, attending
to the outward hiss of traffic on boulevards.
Because the rain is unclear, a vast gray erasing demarcation.
Because the rain makes you tired of the word because,
tired of causes becoming effects, tired of causes, tired of tired reasons.

The Village in the Matchbox

Chatterbox

> *The soul makes the body.*
> —Ralph Waldo Emerson

Walking across the parking lot, I read
a bumper sticker, *Don't drive faster*
than your angel can fly! And then I see
a bag man pushing his shopping cart past
Einstein's, turning his head and speaking
with such animation and hand gestures
and laughter to someone walking alongside
him, who (it takes me a second to notice)
isn't there. Maybe he's driving his cart
faster than his angel can fly but maybe
my angel has flown faster than me
so I only see a man talking to a keen
space above a sunny slab of concrete,
not heat shaping a body from the force
of its companion's character—or do I
mean charisma? Because I am drawn
despite myself to the jovial chatterbox
who strolls abreast his reflection
that contorts in the store's dark glass,
with flashes—too bright—traffic going by, and
I keep recalling nothing nodding yes.

The Village in the Matchbox

cold spring in the Spanish village
spill out the wooden matchsticks
table soft against my cheek
arrange the world the dish

the matchbox is the frame
where rain stars slick the streets
the wrought-iron gate leading to
singing as my hand makes lines

and back up the hill we climbed
the names of things painted blue
at sunset over the stone village
rising from mountains beyond

is a planet Venus and it stands
in the sky except for the sun
shares my tears when I cry
her neck her collarbone warm

where a star floats in the night
her voice makes a lullaby shape
good like my parents' voices
twinkle twinkle little star

I am drawing the stars
when I drink milk from
the sky which spilled me here
so I make sky here with ink

I take the pen from my father's hand
on the white linen spread across the
place where I can let my eye
run away with the spoon

of my drawing the tiny stage
of cobblestone the stairs behind
the grape arbor the nightbird
inside the deep paper going back

where the old church bonged out
purple yellow the sun was a red spot
the houses a stairway to the moon
and the first star my father says

for love is the brightest body
and the moon whose face
in my mother's blouse I love
eyes where I can stay a long time

of her dark eyes I am calm there
on my tongue the sound L tastes
like their names twinkling
how I wonder what you are

and the Milky Way in the matchbox
a blue cup a deep deep blue is
a small child space could swallow me up
make the big little hold it in my hand

the stage where stick figures dance flamenco for the one-legged teacher
clapping hands clicking together the castanets my mother wears red
her skirts are a tree in wind my father wears black a shirt of sun
his boots drum the floor quick quick quick they are so beautiful

I can't see fast enough to hold them dancing around each other like
heavenly bodies orbiting outside the window where rain circles
into rain and a horse tick-tocks by like the castanets' clicking tongues
circling air above the dance floor dangling from my mother's fingers

I am drawing the Spanish village the night cafe you follow my lines
my hand is sure the pen is fine my younger brother runs between
the tables their constellation of families my baby brother sleeps
see Mommy see Daddy see my tiny stage my little dream box

Days of 1964 in Bloomington, Indiana

With kids I was so shy I couldn't speak.
"Turn around and quit staring," they commanded.
My father told me I was beautiful
and they ridiculed my looks: "Your nose is big."
My mother loved my long hair and they asked
if she used it as a mop. I threw away

the sack lunch my grandmother had packed after
they said our food was gross. I couldn't hide
my Greek family, though Mom's proper English
was fluent. When children came to my house,
they twanged, "Whad yer mother say? She tawks funny."
"You got a pin?" meant "Do you have a pen?"

They'd been taught a grammar other than ours.
Brenda and I talked, though. We walked to school
and back, then played together until dark.
Her dad showed us how our hands could create
animal shadows on the wall. A seagull
flew into the night the ceiling held.

Little Bunny Foo Foo bopped the field mice.
The fairy warned him three times to behave—
isn't that right?—his goon face loomed! We yelled
the moral, "Hare today and goon tomorrow!"
Our fourth grade teacher was Mrs. McMillan.
She was pretty, her beautiful blond hair

teased in a French twist. She never had art
when she grew up, so we got something new
each week—finger paints, oil pastels, collage.
Homework was write a poem about the way
a color feels, and I wrote "Blue Is Greece."
Safe places were her classroom, the library,

and home. Late afternoons we filed downstairs
to pick our books. The librarian's helper
had earned a reward for good citizenship.
The chosen boy proudly stamped the due dates.
He had crewcut hair—ugly style, I thought.
"I'm not checking out a book for any nigger."

A grown-up supervised. I can't be certain
if she admonished the boy, "Do your job right."
What I remember most is Brenda's plaintive
question: "I'm not a nigger, am I, Kiki?
I guess she had been spared the word till then,
and I had not yet witnessed it. I answered,

"No, you're not," helpless. Who could free my friend
Brenda from her unchosen role? The only
black child at Elm Heights School. Some say, reflecting
back on those days, "I was ashamed," as if
obliged, as if our color bound us. Brenda
and I stood close, allies. Seeing her hurt,

I felt afraid, more foreign, not shame.
Our friendship was an invisible castle.
Our guests flew in on falling maple leaves.
We divided people into mean and kind.
That boy raised cruel came from the other side
and spoke the language we'd already vowed

never to understand, never to speak.
We held hands in line, waiting to be dismissed.
I can still feel her skin. Our hands were dry
from late autumn. We walked home with no thought
of history, that we'd taken our places,
citizens in the Great Society.

Brenda's mom was fast with grilled cheese sandwiches.
We squeezed on too much ketchup, ate them right up.
Then we kneeled before the window. The sill
was our own stage; the afternoon, our floods.
Our shadowed hands held figurines whom we
moved in a play we made up as we went.

In the Night Box

In the night box is a mess of interstates.
In the glove box are the maps.
Outside the car the dark throbs
like my headache. Mosquitoes and moths

whack against yellow parking lot lights
and buzz the car windows.
They're tiny voices telling secrets
or they're far away newscasters.

Through the windshield kaleidoscope I see
my dad bend over the newspaper box
in truckstop foyer. Then he charms
the girl as he orders coffee.

I read the news today, oh boy.
The Beatles float beside me in the front seat
and we sway together on humid airwaves.
I love them almost as much as my dog.

I'm just a girl but I curl around their rubber soul.
Somewhere on the blue earth is Vietnam.
Radio comes from the sky's brain
and television is a box in its bad dream.

We watch the war over plates
of chicken, rice, and frozen peas.
Soldiers run under helicopter blades,
enormous spinning steakknives.

Faces lolling on stretchers
turn toward the cameras' panic.
Friday nights we read the names
of the dead, scrolling down the screen.

The voice says that's the way it is.
Friends I played pretend with are teenagers
sprawled on mattresses on the floor.
In a few years I want to be like them

and smell of patchouli and making love,
to turn the page that reads war,
be lazy-eyed among inky strokes.
Well, I just had to look, having read the book

where I kiss time right on the lips
with a thousand voices around us
and everyone a fool throwing
the guns and bombs down a big hole.

The ranks of traffic hurl past.
Headlights stars are not stars at all;
maybe people in cars aren't people.
Their bodies are shadows in a box

with no faces, no eyes. You can't even see
the shadows of troops in trucks. They're night sky
over this parking lot, a metallic blank glow,
no color I can name. The war

drives on every interstate across the globe
and my home is flimsy, just a box.
Gunshots mock crickets and fireflies
in our backyard. The gray-blue light

of television blazes into every quiet dark
and into my dreams where the soldiers'
searchlights expose my translucent thighs.
I can't run fast enough to stop seeing My Lai.

How can I wake up? How can I tell
what is near or far when the T.V. taxi
always waits to bear me away?
My brothers sleep on the back seat

and my mother dozes against cool glass.
My father keeps driving until dawn.
A marmalade sky glazes the car
and all my dreams are still real.

At 3:07 A.M.

PUNTA ARENAS, Chile—A wide swath of southern Chile was on alert Monday as dangerous levels of ultraviolet radiation hit peaks because of the depletion of the protective ozone layer over the Antarctic.

Health authorities warned the 120,000 residents of this wool-producing and fishing city—one of the few populated areas beneath the ozone hole in the Southern Hemisphere—not to go out in the sun during the day.

—*The Los Angeles Times*, October 10, 2000

When I get up at 3:07 A.M. to worry and take an antacid tablet,
what pleasure to slip back between the just-washed hands of the sheets
and curl myself around your sleep and feel your belly inflate
against my palm, your skin against my thighs,

to listen for syllables to escape from your dreams,
if only a little "hmm," a question or a sigh,
and to mark yesterday 10/10/2000 the first chill day in the desert,
a small renewal to remember again the sensation of cold wind

pressing itself against me even as the sun scrubs my skin and hair
with a rigorous hot cloth. Why do I have to ruminate now?
Why not give myself to sleep? What are the colors of the moon
crouching behind that cloud in the high window?

What if I count backwards? What about the sheep
who went blind when the ozone hole opened over Chile?
What about the people who can't go outside? What was the question
the night inked on the windowpane when heartburn woke me?

Why is ultraviolet ray pretty to say? Who's next
when those rays kill tiny plants in the food chain? Why do I know
so well the way gravity holds your sweet body on the earth,
your smallest gestures thrilling me, the tilt of your shoulder

as you hold the newspaper, your upturned palm as you exclaim
the story was on the tenth goddamn page of the *L.A. Times*.
Why can't I let the air-purifiers hum me to sleep, take in
the good indoor air, breathe in sync with you and let go?

Why does our daughter's beauty scare me? I wish
you'd seen her this afternoon, her lanky legs running
as she and her friends chased across cultivated lawns,
while crows and sparrows flew up before them

as if to versify their social and bodily joy.
Then she climbed in the car and as we drove
toward home at sunset, she sipped milk through a red straw—
I forgot to tell you this —she said, "Look at the beautiful sky!"

I Don't Grow Wings, I Drive my Car

I drive my car *for that which is ever moving is immortal*
and I keep punching the radio to find the song

to take me back, though I know it's stupid
I want to be moved by a guy who's dead,
playing his guitar like a promise of all
a man's penis can do.

I want to feel it again, right now,
a recollection of those things which our soul once beheld,
when it journeyed with God
my ass gyrating on the car seat.

Socrates says, *Such madness is given by the gods for our greatest happiness,*
and I see the word, "Godforsaken," pass above me, then go by again,
like a memory or the orange planes taking off over the Strip,

over the mountains, one after another, into the same daily blue,
then gone, orange in blue vibrating, dazzling my eye, too much
like what I want, whatever it is, that won't make me happy.

The nose of a plane is phallic.
So is a nose. What does that make
the sky? Socrates doesn't say.

I don't grow wings, I drive my car,
snap my fingers, kiss the sky
beyond the windshield.

The song is *the fourth kind of madness, remembering true beauty,*

moonlit railroad tracks that seemed to meet when they disappeared,
shards of glass and bottle caps that we the lovers compared
to a palace mosaic of sparkling marble in never-ending halls,

because we were stoned and drove
as fast as the car would go,
windows down, pants down,
so much wind and breath,
the getting there was coming—
he receives all service from his lover, as if he were a god.

Yeah, and I got serviced, too, there on the grassy slope
between the tracks and the lake, he knelt before me,
and I pictured myself the guitar he burned
while the party went on in the cabin and the door opened
and raunchy music, laughter, and purple light fell out
with the lonely kid, who puked in the bushes.

Though experience tells me
being high stops feeling good,
still I want to want, I want to fly

as this intimacy continues and the lover comes near
the feathers begin to grow—

I don't grow wings, I drive my car
so he is in love, but he knows not with whom.
I don't grow wings, I drive my car
not knowing which love I remember.

The other souls follow after, all yearning for the upper region
but unable to reach it, and are carried round beneath,
trampling upon and colliding with one another, each striving to pass its neighbor.

So there is the greatest confusion and sweat of rivalry, wherein many are lamed,
and many wings are broken through the incompetence of the drivers.

A man on the corner of Tropicana and Maryland wears sandwich boards,
an Elvis wig and spandex, a white mask over his nose and mouth.

He is another messenger from elsewhere
(or the past) and cannot breathe our poison air.
He sways, waves his arms,
fluttering his sleeves, his sequined wings—

c'mon, c'mon, c'mon, he beckons the cars.
Topless girls, loose slots.
Video poker. Free shots.

He sees himself in his lover as in a mirror. And in the lover's presence,
like him he ceases from his pain, and in his absence,
like him he is filled with yearning such as he inspires,
and love's image, requited love, dwells within him.

* * *

We will now consider the reason why the soul loses its wings.
It is something like this.

The lovers emerge from the bedroom.
The poet takes off, wingspan wide,
into the bright page
having gotten laid.

Even *believing that we have exchanged*
the most binding pledges of love
making love is just a narrative we read and write once,

then urge and urge to reread and rewrite,
and seduction is an invitation to rearrange the same verbs,
lick, touch, kiss, stroke, rub the same body parts.

Because Socrates was not the last to promise the lovers
shall never again pass into darkness and the journey under the earth,
but shall live a happy life in the light as they journey together,
and because of their love shall be alike in their plumage
when they receive their wings.

Here I am, thinking about what we just did,
and I try to feel my feathers stiffen on my shoulder blades,
see if I can flap around the kitchen on my domesticated wings,

looking for something ordinary to shine,
there on the counter, crumbs and unopened mail,
the stain of wine in a glass, images of original bliss.

(Sometimes I notice I'm left out of the dialogue.)

The poet takes off, having gotten laid.
I don't grow wings. I drive my car.

You Play With Yourself

And you imagine playing with another.

You play by yourself and wonder
Who is my imaginary playmate?

You don't know who to put beside you,
Who will play with you, who will be fun.

You love someone, don't you? Think
Of your friend. Oh, but your friend

Won't come to you anymore.
Your friend's not on the playground,

Not on the ground you're on.
Hide and seek, what a good game.

You laughed in each other's arms
To be found. What joy to be found.

Come out, come out, wherever you are.
You won't come without your friend.

You play with yourself. You play pretend.
You think of a friend you knew before.

You had fun, you played well together.
You want to forget your best friend now

Your feelings are hurt. Why does your friend
Keep wrecking the game when you play

With someone else? Keep coming back
But not coming back? It's only pretend.

No one there. No one here. All by yourself
You play with yourself, hide and seek.

Dog Lessons

They who howl with suffering and sirens,
let them snarl a duet with groaning garage-door openers,
with suburban percussion, garbage cans clanging pavement.
Let them teach a lesson to the gates restraining them.
Let them teach the whole damn neighborhood,
they who have got the language of inquiry down-pat.
Who the hell's in trouble now? Who's sick?
Which house a torch in desert sky, the bushes globes of fire?
Let them rise on their hind legs and dance in the dust.
Let them announce strangers and doorbells.
What anguish, what arias in their wild muscular throats
when the UPS guy drives them to apocalypse.
The grumble of his truck's engine. The silly farting brakes.
The unknown is taped up in those boxes.
His brown uniform rubs against itself whispering
awful secrets into the dogs' hyper-alert ears.
Memoirs of the underworld humans cannot hear.

The Velvet Room

It begins with a way to plot
the personal on a velvet wall
I contemplate, as if it were the night

sea churning away from the ferry's hull,
not this moment
in a Manhattan bar,

where I labor against jealousy
burning in each follicle of my scalp,
as he looks at me

too briefly; we meet
somewhere above the amber eye
of his bourbon, and then

he wanders—or does he?—
and I order another drink,
listen to the conversation,

say something clever
for the group, even as the velvet wall
behind his head turns

into the blue-black sea, laughter
into the wake splashing.
I'm leaning into the rail,

heady, breathing the salt and diesel air.
I watch the ship's lighted lounge
over my shoulder—

the bartender's handing two beers
to my lover and the old men smoke, talk,
slap the table to stress a point.

The shopkeeper on her way to Athens
for supplies sleeps in her seat.
Kids' arms and legs hang limp

as clean laundry; their lips
move in dream.
I ask myself why

scheme so elaborately
to keep my secret
from all I know,

as if they cared
or see me stand out
on the deck, waiting for the divine

to unzip, here on the night boat,
here in the bow,
among the coiled lines and anchors,

where I should not be,
though no one can see me feel
his fingers on my ribs,

no one can hear him whisper,
"Scream, go ahead, scream."
No one except him can hear

the glory when I do,
not above the engine's
overwhelming shudder.

Maybe I'd like to
slide away from myself,
now as I contribute my wit

and everyone laughs, I see I
could murmur the wrong words
they couldn't hear,

except him. I could have
smart revenge, couldn't I?
I'm drowsy, numb

to memory and what I want,
having stuffed myself
with virtue and righteousness,

everything seems its opposite,
gluttony, lust, envy—
Scream, go ahead, scream.

Guess What?

You're sitting in an ugly chair.
I can't guess what you want.

What I want isn't guesswork
and it's not my fault

you taunt me or you like to be irked
when I can't read your face.

Ugly words. Ugly space
between our chairs.

No one could guess what was
was beautiful. How about I take off

my dress
in my distress?

or we take a sexy digression
on another question?

as when you lower your voice
and say, "tell me what you want,

it excites me"
(though we disagree,

each in our own despair
in our own ugly chair).

We both want more.
No guesswork there.

Once I wanted space, a vastness
I could travel across.

Now we're estranged
I can't guess how to arrange my life.

Oh, c'mon! Come here!
you say, holding out your arms.

Guess what—I'm worried about harm
and whether I can make it

across the room, that ugly expanse
made plain by our gloom.

Anger

And anger reads my judgment against you.
Your smile is sour and conceals fraud.
I go on and on, watching you from a distance,

as if I were cool behind dark sunglasses
that filtered out the glare of your assessment,
while you repeat evidence against me.

I face your face but close my soul,
turn aside, walk deep into a maze,
go on watching myself, holding you at a distance,

slamming doors behind me (only I can hear).
My anger keeps you blathering inside me,
so I recite again my findings against you.

Yet we sit together at the table, each to serve
the other artfully poisoned morsels, point a fork,
and go on and on, watching the widening distance.

You say, "You should have listened to *me*,"
and, "But *you* had to be *you*, didn't you?"
Then I become the witness who testifies against me.

We deliberate all night, inventing counterpoints,
narrowing our vision at spears of candlelight
and we go on and on, watching from a distance,

as we appeal, go back to discovery, retry, seek
sympathy by recounting suffering and history,
though this defense may deliver the verdict against us:

locked in argument, our embrace will pull us down
through the shades, and we'll hold on to our grievances
and go on, too watchful, unable to get some distance,
reading and helplessly rereading the sentences against us.

A Las Vegas Dust Storm

Out in a dust storm, no one walks the streets.
Heaven is ash and rust. No blue sky plays M.C.
and introduces the Strip to inbound planes.
Look—dust-fall on stucco, tile, pebble, parked cars,
subdivisions bleakly mounting the ruined horizon.

The wind whines, retorts, bargains, scolds,
hurls an orange cone across the freeway.
Palms shake their heads at trembling yuccas
and a warning sign spins across the asphalt.
It's failed talk you don't want to overhear.

Papers fly all around in a fit, newsprint and sex ads—
no white flags of surrender,
though so many young eucalyptus
lie defeated on tract home lawns.
The mountains disappear in a mushroom cloud

of dust, and dust swallows the sun.
Did you know the casinos took busloads
of tourists on atomic picnics? Ah, well.
Who wouldn't want to witness the test
of the ravished world and eat a sandwich?

The Lights of Las Vegas

I'm driving my daughter to the ice cream shop. She's singing along
the words of a song I listened to half my life ago.

No, this isn't a poem about the past. The full moon
that jangled my dreams a couple of days ago is waning now

and the sky is full of planes, those starloads full of people
I can't imagine—can't help imagining—who read

our valley of lights receding beneath the plane, these mercury lights
guiding me down suburban boulevards, a traffic light winking

red to green, these windows lit with televisions and reading lamps,
swimming pools' blue eyes beaming up at the busy freeway of air,

my headlights pushing aside the darknesses so I see asphalt gleam
like a moonless sea though it's only toxic oil and filth,

so I see some rooms from my car because my daughter's singing
a song called "This Flight Tonight" so I can fly off and see

the altar I made in a milk crate, the candle burning and a yellow rose,
postcards of Frida Kahlo's monkey and skull propped up

against the honeycomb of royal blue plastic. Yes, I lay on a futon
on the floor, mourning the end of—I don't want to name it.

I was alone and couldn't sleep. No, this poem isn't turning back.
Outside the rain-sloppy streets hissed a prayer to the tires

who ran over them. Inside I showered till the hot water gave out.
Have you ever tried to end the past? Made a torch of love letters?

I was free on my bed. I could invite anyone to lie down,
and maybe I did. If I slept, I dreamt my bed was outside

where dogs snarled at the chainlink fence and every bark
was a star in my ear. If I cried, the rain didn't let up all day,

all night, all day. If the sun shone, I saw the double clearly
while my dreams walked beside me. There's no self here.

There's no story here. No, this poem won't confess.
This poem is in couplets because it is not about love,

because it knows that form is the body urging
and the mind muttering make love make love make love.

I'm driving to the ice cream store with my daughter.
I see her dreamy look in the rear view mirror as she sings.

Outside the car windows the brightest constellation of stars
is called a flight path. Inside the planes the tourists spot

this valley, a light-spangled carpet unrolling to their hotels,
and they burst out, "Hey, is that the Strip? I can't believe it!"

Here in Vegas nothing is old but the mountains silently observing.
Here is the brand-new ice cream shop. See the patio of concrete tables,

the umbrellas with misting systems cooling the air, parents
sitting on benches while kids press hands to strip mall windows,

yell delight when the owner of the closed toy store
throws open his doors, and all the children run inside

—my daughter, too—and we follow them into the brave new world
where we rediscover spaceships, supermen, baby dolls,

scooters, posters and bath toys and flashcards that teach the alphabet
and how to read. This poem is not retrospective.

This poem is driving home past subdivisions and houses surrounded
 by walls to keep neighbor from neighbor, the desert away from lawns,

automatic sprinklers, and drip irrigation, to block wind and fire.
This poem is half a mile from home where all streets are the same

grid of lights expanding into panic when I lose the narrative
of my driving and my star is one of millions in the galaxy on the ground,

when for a flash of mind I'm stuck in the present with no direction—
sudden monotony, my *now* built of cinder block, stucco, and tile.

to the clock-radio voice, gentle guide who takes your arm
and leads you with such comfortable authority from sleep,
though your dream was a hole in the roof,

> and you wandered the rubble, calling names

> in the merciless damn light

of dream, of waking, too. You want a vague moment, to be quiet gray,
a luxury in-between the skull and consciousness where you lie
under blankets with your sweet one, where shadows stroke your brow,
just as soon you'll stroke your daughter's. Time for school.

> The sun between the blinds

> builds city-states made of dust,

then draws an airborne graph to illustrate the news, some kind of math
you never learned but somehow go on using to calculate the odds,

> the odds of what you fear to say.

> *Happenstance, happenstance,* you chant,

a charm for the daily. The dog thumping *good morning* on the kitchen floor.
The annoying cat. The *click, click, click* that lights the stove. Your surprise.
Your daughter's already awake, and stands naked in the doorway

> when you turn around.

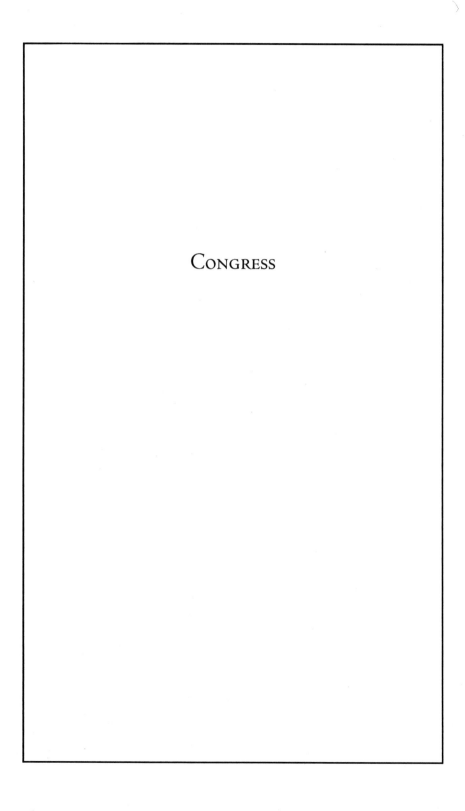

CONGRESS

First Amendment

You shall be free to wander in the woods
and build a fire among the poplars and maples
and worship the face you see in the flames.

If you see no face, you will be free
to pray to fire and give it your own name.

If you lie down in leaves,
if you smell their sweet decay and feel sparks
under the earth, the worms aerating the soil, the seeds
breaking from shells, lifting bald heads to atmosphere,

if you look up to decipher hieroglyphs, the galaxies,
if stars reveal no absolute except abundant randomness,
if you read the book of life and find no law
of nature drafted by a deity, no law shall stop you
returning to the city to broadcast your joy.

If your speech is lawless, you will not violate the law.
If you call on the people to assemble peaceably,
if you unfurl the flags of disposition,
you shall not be dispossessed.
If you petition the government for redress,
you will wander freely nonetheless.

If you build a temple with no cross, no star
but a neon sign proclaiming *No Afterlife,*
no law shall decree religion.
If you print a bible others despise,
your book shall not be abridged.

If you read the oracle,
and you see blood on the teeth of the leader
and if the forgetful legislators stumble behind him,
the hand of law cannot compel you with slap or fist
to alter your grievance. No handcuff, no black boot.
If you assemble words according to your constitution.

Reader

Gently I'll tie you to the mast
So willingly unwilling

You'll be with me
And your ship won't crash.

The cords are made of silk
That yoke your skin to the wind—

Humid sea air breathes now against your cheeks,
Slips in under your clothes

And you relax into my voice
Because it is two palms

Pressing the knots out of your muscles,
A heat surging up through your calves and ribcage.

No need to worry. I've laid my body before
You on a deck chair ten feet away—

And if a breeze lifts up my shirt, reveals
The scar runs down my gut, you'll see the sign

Of past disease is a two-way arrow—
One way points down to sex, one up to heart.

Tell me what you would have me do,
If I could have you—

Only the lull I like, the hum of your valve'd voice
Mellifluously inappropriate,

Wet tongue waking up flesh from the dry dream
Of paper, your forehead lucid with my kisses,

A shivering in the ear's labyrinth, the heft
Of our heads on pillows,

Weight of thighs against listening thighs,
Arch of foot against instep.

Though you're bound with letters, trust me—
I feel you free in my ghost hands

And want to see your face when you come,
When I bend open and enter you.

Ephemeral Ethereal

A couch surrounded by books—
all the furniture there was

in the apartment on Meeting Street.
In Providence the city and streets name aspiration.

Angell and Benevolent are parallel and intersect Benefit;
Hope leads to Prospect and Transit. He read aloud

some ironic passages from H.L. Mencken's I*n Defense of Women.*
There can be no mystery between intellectual equals.

I wanted to hear something else
yet liked his thin fingers on the book,

his bent knee leaned against frayed upholstery,
his expectant gaze when he rose from the text.

It is quite impossible to kill a passion by arguing against it.
Maybe if he'd said *enthralling*

as he fidgeted with his leather belt—
or I would have taken *dissolute.*

But he said, "This thing between us is so—"
and the instant he uttered the syllables

I was lost.
Ephemeral? Ethereal?

One is fleeting; the other, otherworldly—
Which did he say? Which applied to our awkward kiss?

I remember the gas stove flaring up
across the room, a waft of heat,

the geriatric refrigerator moaning
lonely before an expanse of linoleum.

But that learned boy trying to impress me,
what was his name?

Back East Out West With Roger Williams

> *I have not hid within my breast my soul's belief;*
> *although sleeping on the bed either of the pleasures*
> *or profits of sin thou thinkest thy conscience*
> *bound to smite at him that dares to waken thee?*
> —Roger Williams

Out West we say back East, even those who
have never been back East. Out West is out West
because the pioneers broke their wagon wheels
on the Rockies' bones, and the land opened its hands

before them and the sky outstretched wings of air
more enormous than the promise scribed in their minds
or the gold artery concealed in the hills' flesh.
I want to go back East away from the new,

where the sky is small, domestic as a tablecloth
smoothed pretty by God's unbearable lucent hands,
to go to the old city where I was young,
and the Atlantic wind pinched my cheeks,

to be in Providence on Prospect Terrace
where Roger Williams towers over his city,
his hand pointing West toward New Haven,
which is no haven now. I want talk with his ghost

as rain drops cold ink on our faces, to hear him say,
For the broken bags of riches on eagles' wings,
while the hungry jog around a burning trash can.
If it so please the Father of Lights, let in some light...

I want to confide in the heretic Roger Williams,
I live out West, in the city of sin, and drive
on a street named Paradise, in air noxious
with exhaust and dust, where all the boys and girls

play in look-alike homes, no one minds the pleasures
you pursue, and freeway shoots from freeway.
I want to be back East out West and remember
Providence, the mattress on a godforsaken floor,

how I lay believing in the wavering headlights
spreading wilderness on the window glass,
and how I dreamt of the way out West, that always-
out-there tempting faith irresistible even to the faithless.

Her Scarlet Letters

Since the day on the scaffold I have refused
to utter a word that might answer
which father made my daughter's body.

I clothe her with the fiery ink from my needle.
She wears the scripture of my love,
the threads I've wrought of rubies and poppies,

a raspberry stained tongue, the apple heart;
there on her skirts is crimson Eden, my silence
embellished in vermilion, my carmine chant.

She is my Pearl, my scarlet-feathered bird,
she whom the sun flushes with volts of life,
girl made by wildness whom the wilderness loves.

The mourning dove lulls her with its three-note song,
the squirrel gossips from its branch.
The fox and wolf find the dog within them,

lie down for her on a rug woven of moss and leaves.
She is asylum from the congregation;
she the genesis of my exile. I take her hand

and feel paradise in her warm palm,
though I know the doctrine too well.
The flesh is vanity and dust.

And now because she will not say her father
in heaven made her, the dark-minded men of God
want to take her from me, though she exposed

my wayward love. She stands before them
in the light, the twin of my defiance. I see
the window secretly draw a line between her

and the gloomy magistrates. Her guilty
and obscured father looks on. I open my lips,
"Speak for me!" At last I move him

to defend the child born of our consecration;
at last my words embroider the air,
disclosing nothing to the men clothed in black.

On the Eastern Seaboard with Diane DiPrima

Our conversation is in a car because in Greek metaphor
means transport.

We drive the wrong way up a one-way street because we are
too happy to obey the signs.

We pull a U-turn because breath is a U turning and we keep going,
avoiding fatal accident.

We talk about our Calvinist inheritance because we've returned
to our birthplace in the East, though ours were not *a people of God,*

settled in the devil's territories, and we witness
The Wonders of the Invisible World,

more snarled with unintelligible circumstances
than any we have hitherto encountered.

We're stopped by the reborn cops that Cotton Mather
sent after us in our previous lives.

They shout out, Put your hands up! Way up!
and interrogate: Why don't you take Jesus as your savior?

And Diane rounds her fingers
into the reasoning mudra, patiently explains:

to evoke is to call forth something that stays outside yourself
whereas to invoke is to take it inside through the crown.

Then she winks as if *they* were in the know.
And then they let us go.

I say Jesus was a rabbi who thought his word was so smart,
he didn't have to love his mama.

Diane says I'm hungry because the bright body holds the ravenous mind
to her breast while the spirit broods over, flashing her wings.

We order to go. Diane sips milk from a transparent plastic glass,
touches her prayer beads made of shining Chinese coral.

Santosha, santosha chants
the airflow around the windows.

I step on the gas—*Ahhh!*—and we merge
onto the highway, speeding toward Providence.

Children's Literature

On this page, the stranger stands at the screen door,
holding a bunch of tulips wrapped in wet newspaper,
the ink a bruise spreading across his thumb and palm.

"Take them," he says, "I can't stand the sting
of the smeared text. There's no prophesy here.
Give these dumbfounded flowers to your daughter.

Don't tell her they're the color of blood
on her skinned knee. Tell her it's her job
to fill the cobalt vase. Don't forget to say please.

You'll see her delight when she presses
the chair against the cabinets and climbs up.
You'll see her competent hand turn on the faucet,

the water stitching the air with light.
And if you hear an unintelligible murmuring,
don't try to understand. Don't try to read

before your time. Look at the pictures
and take it from there. See, here's a tiny you
scrambling down the bridge of your nose.

You slide down the slope made slick by tear ducts,
stand on the precipice of the brain, tower
above the city built of quartz blocks of sleep,

where the clock tower and the library are ever
under construction, aspiring to reach cumulous clouds.
And there are the cranes and workers in miniature,

enameled toys glimmering in the sand pile—
the planes, taxis, the bank, the hospital, firetrucks,
ambulances, the dumptrucks and bulldozers,

the hands that make the action happen, the child
voice coming from above, making up the story—
this is the scary part—but don't worry—there's a

happy ending. Take these tulips from me, now,
before you turn the page. Let's play pretend.
Let your eyes wander past the newspaper wadded

on the counter. See, your daughter's showing you
she's unwrapped my gift, and she thrusts the red
petals in your face, the wet stems in her fist."

The Storm

I am a girl standing at the screen door
waiting waiting for the cows to come home
mary had a little lamb little lamb
the clouds are a train filling up the blue

with speed and steam the sky is green
the cows glisten on the hill to the tune
of rain of rain my whispered song of *Ohs*
and all the children laugh and play

I think they're a bunch of fools
jumping jumping rope before the bell
I'd bring a little lamb to school
as sun rises filling up a tree with grins

of white teeth strike me down if I lie
to the choir of rain the organ keys of grass
strike me if I stare if I dare keep looking
at lightning racing racing toward me

his white fire hair his wild rose of thorns
wings flame from his shoulderblades and heels
his feet dance on a meadow of bright nails
he smashes the window glass of sky

and strikes me and fills me with his white heat
it doesn't hurt doesn't hurt except the skin
burning beneath the cross around my neck
I am smart and sometimes break the rules

the moon rises huge as the mountains' mouth
now the moon and I dance cheek to cheek
my skin of light against his skin of light
wet grass is lightning under my bare feet

I am a girl standing at the screen door
I breathe in summer's vapor for rainshine
his fleece was white as snow
so is the scar below my collarbone

Alice's Alphabet

Alice is my other name, the alphabet, aerial acrobats flying around me. I
     fall alone into
Blue darkening down the hole inside the book.
C is for curiouser and curiouser. The Cheshire Cat's crazy smile conducts
     me in
Dream to two doors, the diminutive garden where flowers talk and dread
     divorce.
Empty is my eye when my parents are gone. I press my ear against the
     page to hear the story's end.
F is the fear the fawn felt when he woke up to his name and broke free
     from me.
G goes away from Wonderland. I get back with my face in the grass, a
     forest growing above me.
H is leaving home for the Mad Hatter's tea party. The March Hare's
     watch won't tell time.
I is I, tiniest letter for me, my invention in ink.
Joker's wild! makes me laugh, scares me just like the journey.
Kiss me goodnight, Mom and Dad, make it okay.
Lullaby, lullaby, I'm lonely in the looking glass where the
Moon is my face marveling I will grow up.
N is the nonsense I speak at night in the wood where things have no
     names.
O is open sky ringing O globe O orphan in O boat.
P is for the poor mouse swimming in a pool of tears and Alice writing a
     poem where the
Queen of Hearts can't quash her questions.
R is for reading and the reprimanding rabbit. Alice rebels by
Shrinking to speak to the caterpillar, eat soup from a thimble, ride the
     swallow's back,
Travel in a text or a teacup.

U is for union at home.

V is vowing not to forget Alice's voodoo or the village of cards or

Waking in Wonderland with words.

X is for crossing out, for exiting.

Y is yearning, yesterday, a yarn in the yellow yard, where I hold your hand,

Zoë, and we recite our secret alphabet and a zig-zag path opens for us—

Invitation to a Poet

After Elizabeth Bishop

From flat Midwest, over the Rocky Mountains, on this fine evening,
      please come flying.
In a cloud spun of moonrays and rare humid gases,
to the trumpeting of a million horns on the freeway,
descending from the turtle shell of sky,
emerging from the cathedral of mountains,
      please come flying.

The eye of the black glass pyramid watches for your landing
when all the slots will hit the jackpot
and the dealers hand out a royal flush. All the bells
of the wedding chapels will chime out your name.
The invented world is lit up for you. The fountains
of Lake Como dance in greeting. The Eiffel Tower
shares its panorama with your eyes. It's safe to come.
The atmosphere is healthy for the heart and lungs.
The jetstreams of a hundred planes are shaping letters.
      Please come flying.

Come with the pockets of your leather jacket filled
with little lightning bolts and poems,
your shoes filled with the red sand of the Valley of Fire,
the verbs of the long journey chanting from their bending soles.
With visions playing on the lenses of your eyeglasses,
all the ghosts of your ancestors electrifying
the follicles of your hair, riding the back of the winged blue horse
whose shoes trail alphabets through the air,
      please come flying.

Bearing a necklace of angry stars, filling the sleeves
of Pablo Neruda's suit, driving a chariot pulled by scorpions,
with words of salt and sweat burning on your tongue,
		please come flying.
Hotels and schemes blaze in the desert sands; Las Vegas is a mirage
in dry heat and accepts every pleasure this fine evening,
		so please come flying.

Mounting the fleshy breastbone of the canyon with a natural magnetism,
beyond the road rage, crashes, wounded cars and emergency lights,
the billboard whores and flame-breathing magicians,
the metastasizing subdivisions, sprinkler systems and the rows
of haughty palms in shopping mall parking lots,
while the jets and traffic whir in your translating ear
that at once hears a duet of the rattler and coyote,
		please come flying.

A lizard will listen to your lines from the garden wall
and wink at you with her third eye.
With their green sleeves filled with creosote wind,
the arms of the cottonwoods will welcome you as kin.
For whom the starburst, the foot, and the deer scraped into red rock
confide their story, the haunted adobes reveal imperceptible signs,
		please coming flying.
We can string our tears across the room. We can drive fast
eluding all radar or play a game of dangerous communions
with an uncanny set of synchronous pasts
or we can thumb our noses at jealous gods, but please,
		please come flying.

With the language of the hand stroking the earlobes
of the mountains, with nouns growing legs and arms
and dancing all around you,
      please come flying.

Come like a ray of dark darkening the night sky,
come like a midnight sunrise,
with words lifting off the runway in the heat of your arrival,
from the flat Midwest, over the Rocky Mountains, on this fine evening,
      please come flying.

Emily Dickinson in Las Vegas

Throngs who would
not prize them, know
those holy circum-
stances which your
dear eyes have
sought for mine
                        —Emily Dickinson

I don't know me
mirrored in your dear eyes
even when my prized pen
wanders across the desert page
and throngs of birds are
letters to you, their wings

brief imprints on red mountains,
casinos, and resorts that draw
prized throngs to where sun's
big as God's eye—who
knows I seek your
dear eyes, those holy circum-

stances rhymes with dances
can you see an alpha-
bet linking arms by chance,
spinning across world's high-
gloss floor to spell it new
they have changed eyes

who would not prize them
would not want like me
to read your eyes, dear,
the letters, the whys
blooming in fast-motion
on your lens, the throngs

mirrored there among the growling
cars, the freeway's wild
dogs, chaos so bright
the throng's mesmerized—even the moon
sees the night city
the eye of the black pyramid

shooting megawatts into space, prizes
for throngs—the jets' contrails
announce the sequined bride
the groom's throat surgeon-scarred
the ruby tongue stuttering
what God has brought together

in ten rented minutes—holy
the wedding chapel—let no
one tear asunder—say
I love you, common words
and seek me uniquely—making
love hits the jackpot

ask your throbbing Scripture
how to follow the letter
the chance spirit, how
to read what your dear
eyes have sought for mine
in Las Vegas or the meadows

throngs pray to be chosen
in the jasper-walled casino
Lord and Lady Luck stand knowing
holy circumstances, the slots' electronic
music chanting *bing bing bingo*
luring hope for the prize

Ode to my Hair Stylist

For she takes me back to adolescent joy when she colors my hair the exact dirty blond, with its natural highlights and lowlights, that it was when I was seventeen.

For she will let me keep my gray steak with grace.

For when I say I've earned my white hairs, she will nod with utter compassion and incomprehension.

For she shushes the stylist in the next station when she gossips that at forty the client who just left is old.

For she knows I have a sympathetic ear.

For she circles me in a rite to the goddess whose voluptuous plaster form oversees the proceedings.

For she is surrounded by other beauties and her temple is laden with talismans for the idol.

For she has made her hair healthy as a vestal virgin's with curative herbal ingredients in priceless shampoos, conditioners, and leave-in treatments.

For aroma therapy makes me sneeze.

For she sells a magic cream to heal wrinkles, itches, and zits.

For she offers to make my headhairs and pubes match.

For her breasts don't sag beneath the rhinestone logo on her t-shirt.

For her powdered cheeks glitter with tiny ersatz sparkles of sand and sun.

For her layers of foil render me an Egyptian princess, a Cleopatra or a Berenice.

For her dizzying potions and dyes hypnotize me though the oracle is invisible.

For her daughter's father is not drug-free and he brings the girl home late from visits despite the court order.

For the owners of the salon are unkind.

For she has no health insurance.

For she could have gone to college were it not for her stingy father.

For I ask the outraged questions she expects and raise her pedestal higher.

For her problems are not my own.

For she hands me fashion magazines and saves me from work.

For she feigns she shares my taste in clothes.

For she slowly steps round me in silk harem slippers and undulates her
    arms above me like a belly dancer.

For she rhythmically massages my head and neck under a stream of
    skillfully adjusted warm water and she lulls me into a dream of
    ease.

For she has hidden her every imperfection.

For she blow-dries my hair into a confection of hairspray and pomades I
    could not reproduce.

For her favorite part is the closing ceremony, when she spins the chair to
    show me my back in the mirror, the beauty I cannot see.

Catherine and Eva

After John Berryman

1.
Catherine says: I love to love a blank page,
a white room, empty, except three shapes
on which my mind can dwell, a sea-scrubbed conch,
a calla lily—flower unfurls from stem but divulges
nothing—a silver goblet is a mirror: the inside
floats my mask on wine; the outside

contains my hallucination, all plural:
spirals on its polished surface,
my biography in lowercase.
My trifoliate mind coils and recoils,
never wants to veer from pure and small
contemplation, from the prism Eva calls

prison. She's a verb and I'm a noun
lounging on clean linen.
She winces at stillness. Her high velocity
impinges on the pale hour when I am near
vanishing as I peel an orange. In my hand are pretty
details—sweet topaz, infinite, tiny. But being is austere.

2.
I want to make her scream, says Eva, murmur
sodomy in her ear. I've got olive oil in my palm.
A zipper, then wham. I can quake sterner
even than Catherine in bowtie. The body's tantrum
is raunchy, musky like rosemary crushed.
I want to tease her from dumb calm,

vibrate her giddy as a tuning fork. I say
delectable and the syllables are a lover's
tongue in my mouth, sensate,
playing on the verge
of being skin, then skin against skin, the covers
kicked off when we answered

need. I'm always disheveled, my scarf's awry,
my jacket, unbuttoned, fills with the wind
that moves me toward some *you*. We'll roll
in wet constellations, half-naked, sly
beneath or behind something. I can't stand
her loneliness. Give me color, chaos, loss of control.

Civil Disobedience, New Year's, 1980

When the clock stuck 12

                                  I wept

"Why should a number matter?" I asked David

                      All my lovers were named David

Nice Jewish boys born in the '50s

                "Why discount your premonition?" he replied

"A number is a symbol

                          Like a word or a rose

Of poison plutonium"

                He took my hand and stroked it—thin thin

Fingers made tracks of emerald neon

                  Across my palms—circled my wrists

Like Chinese jade a woman wears

                          For safety

One on each arm—so the jade breaks—not her—if she falls

                        He'd been in jail

As if I were mere flesh and blood and bones

                To be locked up. . . .if there was a wall

Between me and my townsmen

                There was a still more difficult one

To climb or break through—he'd cut a fence

                At Seabrook nuclear plant

Been beaten been gassed

                  He was already thin

When he went on a hunger strike

                There was a history and a gossip

Which never circulated

                Beyond the walls of the jail

# # # # # #   # # # # # # # # # # #

\# \# \# \# \# \# \# \# \# \# \# \#

"David" I said "you're so thin your body's

                      A stick holding up a head and a penis"

My boyfriend in the other room

                  Nursed Jack Daniels and beer and heavy visuals

The acid was bad

                       Cut with strychnine—tore

A black hole in my temple

                  A dizzy galaxy spun on my tongue

Between walls of clenched teeth

                  Before they could get to be as free as I was

I knew I would never be fully his

                     Whose? not anyone's

Not for another decade at least or ever

                  I did not for a moment feel confined

The years split away from their orbits

                  Asteroids that lay weight on my chest

They thought my chief desire was

                  To stand on the other side of that stone wall

In New England everywhere you see walls

                    Boulders placed with care

Convex against concave like hip and hip

                  And you attend to their form

Read across and then down

                  The word shapes becoming stone shapes

The lines becoming walls

                  Around you and around you is

A page—a map—a city is Providence

                  Where verses are composed, which are

Afterward printed in a circular form

                                Where you walk down Hope Street

Parallel to Benefit

                                     And intersect with Prospect

And Angell *and the walls seemed a great waste*

                                       Of stone and mortar

I said "it's the shapeless that frightens me

                             The gas in the air—the waste

With infinite half-lives"—my boyfriend

                       Was on the other side of the wall that much

Was certain—I heard

                                        I will breathe

After my fashion

                          The click click click of the Bic

As he lit a joint or a cigarette named Viceroy

                   I saw smoke angels take wing and mingle

With Mahavishnu Orchestra's tolling

                 And the little cockroaches dotting the walls

They only can force me

                          Who obey a higher law than I

And I saw the wall of me permeated by what

                           Could not be locked up

He occupied one window

                               And I the other

My boyfriend looked in

              He asked "when was the last time you were this high?"

I had never seen the town-clock strike before

                   Then he stabbed the rose on the album cover

Three times with his finger and I mused

                 Was David king or prophet or schemer or singer?

Who had been detected in an attempt to escape

Who avenged themselves by singing

Yes for a moment I could read the signs

                                              If I recalled

Hip rhymes with lip—skin thin—bug hug

                              "Don't cry damnit" said my boyfriend

"Don't mess with my high"

                                        I could not but smile

To see how industriously they locked the door

                                          On my meditations

Which followed them out again without let or hindrance

                                      Any David would do

No it was more

                      David was David—the one—the seven—the twelve

The beautiful—the pure

                                 One hand stroking my hand's

Innumerable cells and cells

                          And cells as I touched him innumerable

David—one hand cocked and grasping a stone

                                     One hip cocked

The giant grotesque and leering

Idealism

Emerson, what if you are right? Maybe
you hand me a plastic vial of anti-depressants

or maybe you stride over to the radio mumbling
in the background and turn the volume up so loud

my skull feels like a china sugar bowl
shattered against asphalt. "What opium

is instilled into all disaster!" or else
the structure of the mind collapses with experience

and the television images replayed, the slow falling
towers and fast falling people, the voice calling out

"Oh, my God!" The oversoul is splayed above
the mountains' dark silhouette, a metallic sheen

above the airport's happy neon and its bright spiraling
parking garages. It crosses the windowpane every minute,

rides in on the wings of jets, carries in the rancid air
from New York, the terrible ash from Washington.

I can't help it, when I breathe, I smell the space
between souls—Emerson, is this what you meant?

The print on the page is the form, each letter
a part of a body, an arm, an eye and half a nose,

a leg and a penis and a pocket with a wallet
and money the owner can never spend, something to give

to the family, to identify the loved parts of a man.
Dear God, how can I reattach all this to the whole?

The words are the people when they stopped all the cars,
taxis, and trucks and got out. They stood all together

on the streets and all together they gasped
as they laid their hands on their hearts.

I wanted to make something beautiful to recall
you, Emerson, "Grief too will make us idealists."

If I could concentrate on one thing or one life,
one name or one face, perhaps I would ascend

the stairs you speak of, would see God's hieroglyph
written on the wall. I am afraid of heights

and don't want to see with God's fire-filled eyes,
don't want to "die out of nature and be born again

in this new yet unapproachable America."
Yet I want you to be right, if only I could see

with no pain-killer at all, if I could meet
a soul, if I could touch arms made of smoke.

In the Optometrist's Waiting Room

After Elizabeth Bishop

In Las Vegas, Nevada
I took my daughter with me
to pick up my new glasses.
We sat together and waited
for my name to be called.
It was spring. It stayed light
late. A man in white pants,
long legs crossed at the knees,
lounged near the plate glass store front,
the sun on his content face.
My daughter picked up *Time*
(she could read only a few words)
and, before I saw which magazine
she held, she carefully
studied the photograph:
a naked boy lying in bed,
shot from the side
so the viewer can see his right arm
blown off, the stub of his shoulder
bandaged, the skin of his torso
burned, a terrifying chaos
of black and white and gray,
nothing like the color of skin.
He rests his right cheek on the pillow
and his eyes meet the lens.
A woman in a black hijab
stands in the left wing of the frame,
head bowed, looking down at him.
"Mommy, what's this?"
my daughter asked.

Suddenly, from inside me
came an *oh* of pain
—my voice, in my chest—
which I suppressed to protect
my girl and I explained the boy
lost his arms to a bomb in the war.
"But Mommy, what's this—
on his stomach?" and I explained
that (that uncolor, that mass) was
his skin where he had been burned.
I kept talking—measured, maternal—
my hand on her forehead. She tilted
her head back a bit to meet my gaze
and despite all my effort of thought
she was the boy,
her matchless skin was his.
"Please, don't look anymore," I said,
and our hands together closed *Time*,
placed it on top of the pile. I noted
the cover photo of the smiling dictator
surrounded by red margins and type,
the date, April 21, 2003.

I said to myself two days ago
she turned six years old.
I was saying it to stop
the sensation that the desert sun
cast in slants across the window
was bursting shards and fire.
But I felt: she is an *I*,
she is a *Zoë*,

she is one of *them*.
Why should my child be one, too?
I could hardly bear to see
the image developing in her mind
as she sat beside me, her exposed knees
resting on the chair cushions,
there in the friendly eye doctor's office
where posters show beautifully
bespectacled families smiling
and placards politely request you sign in.
I knew our strange feeling for a stranger
was familiar, and would happen again.
Why shouldn't my daughter be me
or her or the boy or anyone?
Shouldn't our similarities—
knees, eyes, the family hands
I held in my lap, or even *Time*
and that appalling burned skin—
hold us all together
and make us all just one?

"C'mon," I said, "Let's try on glasses for fun."
And we modeled the luxury frames,
faces grinning together in clean mirrors.
The magnanimous doctor came out
to chat and encourage
while his assistants handed us more
options and offered opinions.
"We're all so silly," I said to Zoë,
"you don't need glasses to see."

The technician carried my new frames
in a tray. I looked out the store window
at the boulevard, my vision restored to 20-20.
The waiting room was too air-conditioned
and whirled with the cars rolling by
in bright wave after wave flashing light.

Then I was back in it.
The war was reported over. Outside
in Las Vegas, Nevada
were sun, no clouds, and hot asphalt,
and it was still the twenty-first
of April, 2003.

BRIGHT BODY

Applause on the Beach

Applause, applause for this calm hour,
when small waves breaking on the shore are hands

lightly clapping along to murmured song,
the hour before suppertime, before

the sun drops a red grape into the open-
mouthed mountains. I taste sweet heat and salt-

water electric in my every pore
when I dive in. Across the sea's expanse,

my daughter's face concentrates on play.
The sun running its fingers though her hair

she pays no mind as she shovels fine sand
expertly into a lime-green bucket

and mortars in her castles' spiraling wing.
I can't discern all of her narrative.

She sits cross-legged in the moat, enthroned,
the naked, perfect queen, ruling a beach emptied

of subjects, with her staff a plastic rake,
her skin bejeweled with sand, seaweed, and ice cream.

Yellow Letter

Today I want to paint the color yellow,
the East, chrome fields of wheat flowers
receding into hills, new grass,

a sign before the farmhouse, gold-edged,
Give us this day our daily bread.
Forsythias' tangled heads blooming

beside the Old Groves Mill.
It was the old world, still orderly,
everything arranged for generations.

They knew to mind their manners,
the terms of exchange.
I want you to see their labor,

the water wheel turning,
liquid stars shoot into the spring sky,
the farmers trading some grain for milled flour.

Write to me.

* * *

Now when you walk the streets where we began,
when the past speaks as memory does without propriety.

After years in California I went back East.
I was trying to find the design of events,
why people say it was meant to be—

I leaned my cheek against the cold car window
to cool the flush of remembering the Berkeley hills
and making love under live oaks.

Your tongue is sun—

You sang loud as we descended
into the city and the social,
ambled down stairs set in the hill,

naked beneath our clothes,
and the afternoon withdrew
into the redwoods' damp shade.

Your index finger inscribed spirals on my spine
so I'm painting the stanza window electric
like the window of the house we passed

where someone playing piano harmonized with your song—

I'm drawing an aerial map
of our conversation, the gilded bridges
spanning the bay

when you said something about a call
and a phone rang like a punch line.

San Francisco was a vast ship
passing through the Golden Gate.

Amber lamps glittered below in the dark flatlands.
Twinned headlights coursed down Telegraph.

* * *

Look at the paper.
Watch now as I dip my brush
in cadmium and the sun

bursts in water and rivulets flash
every which way on the page.
Is it moving close to you or pulling you

away, to the horizon?
Yellow's nature is to bewilder, I guess,
just like our correspondence, my friend.

Follow yellow sign to yellow sign inside the picture
where the signs are lost and who we are
can intersect again:

a boy in a yellow T-shirt and yellow shorts
walks by the yellow fire hydrant.
His lanky limbs move through heat

and I can feel him feel the bulk of air, the weight of flesh.

He's the brightest on the street, a shining answer. You.

Your Name Is the Boat

His name is the boat . . .
　　　—Mira Bai

I laze in a boat, my way in the wind's hands.
　　　—Wang Wei

your name is the boat and I am saying your name into the wind's hands

your hands are a boat and my skin is the wind filling up your sail

I laze in the boat of your body my way in your breath's hands

our windy hands push our boat across our names written on water

I am the boat and lazing in my hull you are my way to lose my name

my name is the boat and you are in me and you are rowing us across

you are rowing me rowing me rowing me across to you

you are the oar and I am the water you row

your name floats on my slippery skin and disappears deep in my waters

Macho Wind

Some say they like the wind.
Yes, it's grand, a bully who flexes
big articulate muscles and keeps
the ships in port for three days.

He does all the talking, swaggers
down the streets, a real virtuoso
when he hisses and yowls and bangs
a syncopated beat with the shutters.

I guess if he bit the nape of my neck
I'd swoon, or if he threw me against a wall
and lifted my skirt,
I'd shiver for his chilly fingers.

For a while the jealous wind insists
I give him all my thoughts—
slams a chair across the square
if my fantasies stray. Then he sneaks off

to kick up trouble elsewhere.
In stillness all is untouched by his visit.
I take my pleasure to the beach
and lay myself bare for the sun.

Elegy for a Lover Of Horses

I will not forget the light of the horses.
—Pablo Neruda

(for Elvie Dublin)

Her horses came to us and laid their heavy heads
      on our shoulders and we slow-danced,
looked into their polished and enormous eyes
      and floated on the lakes of their eyes.

Bitter vegetable horse smell.
      Sun gleamed in the gaps between the slats of her barn,
studded the interior with topaz,
      changed hay from melancholy to yellow.

"Two things I wanted to know," she said,
      "the human psyche and the animal."
And she held the colt, one arm about his neck
      one hand on his forehead.

"Yes, baby," she said. "Yes, darling I know."
      Her horses circled inside the barn in a dance
of blood and rhythm, amber muscles flickering,
      hooves crushing mist.

Her horses came to us and asked us to lay our ears
      against the warm slope of their necks and listen to the calm
pulsing within them. The sun came in
      the barn door without even knocking,

then burnished the horse's flanks orange and childlike drew
  a star at the tip of each ear.
Winter bit us with diamond teeth.
  Now planes take off into mountains,

one a minute, with the upswing of a metronome.
  I walk in desert dust, sharing glassy sun with hotels,
past cypress, pine, and Joshua trees, past ranches
  with pick-ups and SUVs shining in driveways.

She comes toward me as slowly the horses approach
  and nod their heads over the fence,
as if she's invited them to me,
  she from the light of horses departed.

Making Love After Catastrophe

The ghosts of the people killed crowded into our room,
each one a rainbow where skin would be,
and some slid along us, the women and the men,
sharing in our bodily bliss, passionate with us,
as if they lived. Some swam in the air
between the bed and the walls, and between
our breaths I could hear their longing.
The children hovered in the corners silently
and saw what they would never know
and I saw their little mouths were only
glimmers moving without words now,
their lips a dark without a kiss.
The dead crowded into our room, like light twisting
on the surface of night waters, they made love
with us, they wanted us and to be an *us*, wanted
to be flesh against warm flesh, wanted to hold
the beloved and pleasured body close again.

My Friend Steve Asks if I Believe in the Afterlife

—Catherine Ellen Chirls died September 11, 2001 WTC

When the boy delivering her eulogy
first uttered "mother," a baby sparrow
landed on his head. The boy reached up
and took the bird in his guardian hand,

felt the heart's quick pulsing and the uncanny
feathers against his skin, the heat
and smoothness of the small body.
Then he opened his hand like a single

lonely wing and set her free, there
before the hundreds of gasping mourners
and *The New York Times* reporter
who made her visitation fact.

I would become a bird to reach my child.
How could I not come if she called?
How else explain the sparrow that defied
instinct? A mother's soul would ask

to borrow a body for a few seconds,
to remind her son, "Never limit yourself,"
as she did one night, the newspaper tells us,
as they cleaned up after supper.

Yet I can't help thinking how cruel
to let a parent soul stay long
in a sparrow's body, never to speak
a word to her son or touch a cheek

he's just begun to shave. Maybe
in the zoology of mourning
the winged creatures fly to our need
and cross the border from the wild

into human memory, which might be
the afterlife—the strange word afterlife
tells the time after death when a sparrow
is mercy perched on a boy's head,

is mother for an instant, then flies off,
identical to others in her species, gone
in the evergreen filling with autumn wind,
like a feathered breast taking in breath.

You Hate Windchimes—

an illness ringing under your skin,
        the past's awful music
            silencing your appetite,
    a daily waking too early,

    and you walk from room
to room and insist,
    I still have a body,
            while the wind goes on
    adamant: listen

to your bones clink,
clink, clink
        far away from you, somewhere
in dusty air. Your isolated ear hears
despite you.

        And you feel what
you're bid,
can't help yourself, when
you taste trauma in your spit
and you smell what happened then,

someone trying
            in vain to make
home and garden
            sweet,
the same five notes randomly played.

A Body Politic

When you don't eat all day,
the empty wind fuses
with your exquisite anger,
moans in your lonely gut.

If all you see appears ill-lit
and you stumble a bit,
you haven't lost your verve
because you are upset

and not dressed in rags
like the child as deserving
as you who held out
her hand in Katmandu.

You are hungry enough
to watch your anxious
cells in combat. And if
fasting makes you sleepless

you'll be depleted yet
nourished luxuriously
by a reserve of fat,
and you'll get up

unsteady, not yet ready
to seek the vengeance
your seething body
wants to exact.

Photo Op

I have a headache in this photograph
though I am gazing upward like a saint
in rapture, listening to God's blurry words
written with cigarette smoke, ornate deadly font.

Okay, so I hold a lily in one hand
and an apple balances on the other palm,
but it was for effect, so forget
you saw the poet with the lily and the apple

even as a joke. My picture
needs some underlying fear.
As if in prayer, my hands are folded
on newspapers and magazines

arrayed across the table as if in disarray,
a bit out of focus, yet working
on you just the same. Notice
the open-mouthed head stilled above me

on the TV, the frames within the frame
that inform you, the orange terror alert
and the headline ticker scrolling along
the bottom of the screen—

news, weather, stock prices, pollen count—
everything fit for you to know,
familiar and alarming.
See, in this shot my pen is poised just so

and in my expression you might detect
I'm a bit proud to say—"ouch, my head
hurts from looking at God knows what—"
the emblems dovetailed with feelings so deftly,

we can't help the tears or wanting to kiss
the icon or the idol, can't help anything at all—
the composition is crowded with too much:
radiant graininess where I dusted for evidence

of the maker's fingerprints, the extreme wide angle
revealing my background, halos inlaid
around the masses pressing toward heaven,
though their feet tread on the heads

of the wretched who carry their few worldly goods
in a cloth sack, and a thin baby,
or pull on the hand of the knock-kneed child
who stares you down no matter where you stand—

you'll find them here, in the bottom corner,
turned away at the border, where smoke rises,
whether from the fire of war or holy incense,
impossible to tell, there's too much damned noise.

Take a Deep Breath

Of course, you are afraid to breathe—of what
enters you if you inhale fully—smoke
seeps from the car beside you. When you stop

for red you slyly observe the couple breathes
together. Cigarettes punctuate their speech,
their bodies slouched against the gray interior.

The cars idling ahead of you exhale
too much. The sun is filtered by exhaust,
exhausting you. You think of what is next

to do and squeeze the steering wheel and hold
your breath, aghast you can't help that you find
the gasses lovely, belly-dancing there,

beckoning and winking and wriggling
on asphalt between puffing, lustful cars
that sit expectant on their fat asses, drunk

on our velocity, oh holy God—
what if you felt your body and what if
you took a breath, the living form of it

inside you, and you felt the ghosts of cars
inside you, too, the giant neon guitar
outside the Hard Rock Café on the corner

of Paradise twanging amid your ribs,
and all the splendor of inanimate
objects left you just as they entered you.

What if the couple enclosed in the car
were no longer ugly to you and all
the oxygen coursing in our blood

made you love them for an instant, made them
perhaps glance over at you, perhaps not.
The light changes to green, adorned with halos

of toxins. You look down at your splayed legs,
admire them, too. A pity you're impelled
to take a breath, step gentle on the gas.

Close to Death

We sped for hours to the hospital.
"I feel weak," I said to my alarmed father
who looked at me with fearful love, as if
I were vanishing there into my thinness.
How many times we talked and talked on drives.
We didn't have so much to say this trip.
I leaned my head against the frozen window.
The day was gray—across the snowy plains,
a plot of light. I thought it was not death's
bright body as they say. What was to stop me
from going inside the gray? Those were also
the wrong words. "I" would no longer be,
so could not "go." Could vague become more vague?
I asked myself: if I can't eat, can't drink,
how will I live? The answer was too clear
there in the roadside diner where my dad
had stopped for coffee and I saw the people
eating and drinking their colorful meals,
the eggs glowing with grease, ketchup a poppy
adorning the white plates alongside hands
that held up sunny vials of orange juice
like hope, replete with anti-oxidants.
They were swallowing the good nutrients,
and I wished I could, too—how ordinary!
I saw formal beauty is normality:
think of regular features, regular meals,
regular heartbeat. If the body were
ordinary, the self might live and be
extraordinary.
       And therefore I donned

a hospital gown, became a patient,
a no one observed under a spotlight.
The doctor said, "No doubt she is too thin,"
when they wrapped the blood pressure cuff around
my arm twice, then stuck me with a cold IV.
I watched my father's face as I was wheeled
away, remembered my child's expression.
But could I will my body to live for them?
I lay alone, cold on the narrow gurney,
and close to death, as if one could be close
to nothing, to the ceiling's nothing, or walls,
or mortar between bricks. The nurse came in,
smiling, my anesthesia on a tray.
"You'll be awake but you'll feel no pain.
You'll forget it all." And then I went under
to float awhile on Lethe, and I wondered
on which bank would I land, recalling what?

When I Think of the Hand

of God I think
of my little daughter's hands
imitating her father

pressing pain from my back
with familial oil
then affliction slips

from my shoulders
disappears in the underworld
are you better now? she asks

as if she were mother
her hand pushes hair from my forehead
and heat runs though my body

and it encircles the three of us
as if we were in safe hands
as if as if as if

the hand of God were to reach
from the big nothing where the galaxies end
and pull the bombs back

and squeeze them in his fist
and fling a new star up into the ether
before the bombs hit land

before the wedding party disperses
its festive clothes aflame
a little brain among the grasses

a child's shoe lost in Baghdad
wanders inconsolable
looking for its mate

as if the soul
could petition for the wholeness
of its flesh

Days of 2003

Here's a minute of my jubilation before the blue dwindles
and falls to the flowers of the desert willow
and falls onto the boulders on the mountain summit.
She'd been riding her bike in the park, tracing a helix
on the sidewalk that runs through the grass, a fiction
of a lawn, really, a little heaven made by sprinklers.
Her index finger is hooked in the collar of her princess t-shirt.
She smiles at me, off-guard, just for an instant
before losing patience and running from the camera,
climbing on a swing, stretching her strong legs to the sky,
before we get in the car to go home for dinner,
before I think, "count your blessings," and am ashamed.
As if we were chosen. Here's a picture of my daughter
just before the sun sinks, igniting fires along the borders
of a purple cloud. Here's a day, and our ordinary luck.

A Field of War

"One Tree," encaustic on panel, 36 x 24, 2002,
by Felicia Van Bork

One tulip tree
lets out a few spring buds,
unfurling new green flags.

One white-barked sycamore
seems reticent,
a leafless ghost.

One tree in winter,
one in spring, two trees
together passing time,

making your logic that goes
from A to Z then to I and Y
or K and B simply

because the letters are pretty
or begin a name or a question
or recall two trees,

sentries before the barn
in a field where you grew up,
where the woods on the horizon

are rich impasto, a tangle
of fleshy lights and smells
of the land waking up.

The small barn door in the right corner
is open, revealing purple
gloom and enough brightness

to invite you inside. The door's shadow
draws you in
to what is not in the picture.

* * *

You and your first love have stolen away
and lie on a blanket spread on hay.
We've come, he says, to think.

So you think what to think. Light caught
in the cracks between the slats is wax beads
dripping down a candle.

You breathe in the blanket,
the hay, his white embroidered shirt
his prudish mom washed,

and you find not
one thought
because you've smoked pot

and made love not war.
The war is on
nearly as long as you can remember

You lie together, eye to eye in the barn,
thinking what to think.
The development they'll build

after they tear down this barn
where you lounge stoned and newly fucked
will be called Sycamore Knolls,

yet they've bulldozed the old and stately trees,
and they lie on the ground, limbs curled in
to their trunks. Outside, bulldozers stand at ease,

alone with the barn in acres of mud, red clay
that sticks to the bottoms of your shoes
and accrues and weighs you down as you trudge.

* * *

Now your shoes and his shoes are mudcaked,
stuck with hay, hastily untied, kicked-off, askew,
filled with ghosts of you, the vandals

who pulled up all the surveyors' stakes
in the field that despite you will be
houses and driveways on streets

named for what they destroyed to build:
Sycamore, Meadowbluff, Fair Oak.
They destroy the village to save it.

That's what they say.
His devout and patriotic mother checks
the odometer before lending him the Beetle

that's too small for sex
but here you are, lying in her altar boy's arms,
his sperm swimming inside you, futilely.

In a year they'll draw his birthday in the lottery,
his number come up, high or low. You don't know
by then they won't call more men.

He's just a boy,
the prettiest boy you've known, so far,
and your fingers stroke his temple

and the corner of his eye with no crow's feet.
You feel yourself in time and you can't think.
You won't think how to keep his face perfect

as a funerary portrait
made of translucent layers
of pigment and beeswax,

the encaustic startlingly young, like the flesh you touch
infused with his cobalt gaze,
his injunction to think.

You want him like this—his eyes moving
with his hand from your hair to your hip,
drawing you in

to a danger not pictured
and words winging with the swallows
up high in the skeletal rafters of the barn.

Freeway Love Poem

Tonight these lines talk to me and you.
I don't know what will come next. Listen

to quiet and to the sad, waning moon
covered in dreary veils. I understand

her lonely countenance, her gravity,
there above the billboards' come-ons,

the woman lounging in a black lace bra
before a platter of sushi, and ready

to share her fleshy feast, the illumined
icons of the Wheel of Fortune, promises

of riches and luck for all the unlucky
speeding crazily across

each others' lanes, desperate for their exit,
regardless, regardless.

Oh, I know better than to converse
with the moon or call it a *she*,

claim to understand its expression,
which is just craters on a sphere of stone.

Because I'm in a vehicle flashing along
the utopian freeway to a new tenor

of thought. The radio's off. And I listen
to something I call *myself*

when I should be erasing *I,* should be
shutting those voids, the moon's eyes.

I love you. You question
whether the soul has a mate.

I take the back way home,
to the extent there is a back way,

still some dark spaces,
where shadows

of horses rock on desert dust under
only a few streetlights in a city

that shines brighter than the moon, my love,
where nature barely exists in our racing

minds, where epiphany is a projection
onto a gray screen or billboard maybe,

biochemistry or a fluke of genetic
inheritance. Yet I love you, though love

is dumb. Dum de dum dum. Doomed and loony
old moon (I mean me). I'm too sensitive

to sounds, which I adore and make me mad.
I can hear what you're *not* saying. Say it,

damn it. Because, as the saying goes,
to close the distance between us,

I'm driving too fast, driving to the end
of my poem or the road

home (as if there were one), though
I want no end, no closure.

I listen for you to come close, your soul
to speak out of nothing or things I see—

supermarkets and full parking lots
below the persistent moon

that keeps following along.
I can almost feel you in my breath,

my solitary breath, boxed in by glass.

NOTES

You Pray to Rain Falling on the Desert: Quotation is from Exodus 6:6, when God speaks to Moses.

Days of 1964 in Bloomington, Indiana: Bloomington, Indiana had segregated elementary schools until 1954. The school system didn't hire African-American teachers until 1963. When I was in elementary school, there was probably defacto segregation, I'm guessing. I'm sure that Brenda was the only black child at Elm Heights when I was in the third grade.

I Don't Grow Wings, I Drive My Car: Quotations are from Plato's *Phaedrus,* translated by Harold North Fowler.

Guess What?: One of the projects that the Dutch furniture designer, Gerard Vollenbrock, assigns his students is to design an ugly chair.

First Amendment: The constitutional rights guaranteed by the First Amendment—the freedoms of religion, speech, the press, peaceful assembly, and to petition the government for redress—are embedded in the poem.

Reader: "Only the lull I like, the hum of your valve'd voice," Walt Whitman, "Song of Myself" (line 86).

Back East Out West with Roger Williams: Quotations are from Roger Williams' *The Bloody Tenet of Persecution, for the Cause of Conscience, in a Conference between Truth and Peace.*

On the Eastern Seaboard with Diane di Prima: Quotation is from Cotton Mather's "Wonders of the Invisible World." In the yogic tradition, Santosha (contentment) is one of the five *Niyamas* (rules of conduct).

Civil Disobedience, New Year's, 1980: Quotations are from Henry David Thoreau's "Civil Disobedience."

Idealism: Quotations are from Ralph Waldo Emerson's "Experience."

My Friend Steve Asks if I Believe in the Afterlife: I thank Steve Huff for asking the question that inspired this poem.

A Field of War: "We had to destroy the village to save it," is an infamous quotation of an unnamed Army officer, in 1968, during the Tet offensive. It may refer to the massacre at My Lai.

"They'll draw his birthday in the lottery." During the Vietnam War, in 1969, the Selective Service reinstituted the lottery, in which the birthdays of all men born in a given year were drawn. The lottery determined the order in which men were called to report for induction into the military, so the lower the number the more likely a man was to be called. The last lottery was held on February 2, 1972, for men born in 1953, and who would have been called in 1973. However, no new draft orders were issued after 1972.

The Author

Aliki Barnstone is a poet, translator, critic, editor, and visual artist. She grew up in Bloomington, Indiana, and spent summers in Brandon, Vermont. Barnstone was educated at Brown University (A.B. and A.M.), Middlebury Language School in Spanish, the University of California at Santa Cruz, and the University of California at Berkeley (Ph.D.) She has taught at Beloit College, Marquette University, Bucknell University, the University of South Dakota, the Prague Summer Program, and was writer-in-residence at Villanova University. From 1999–2007, she was Professor in the Department of English's International MFA Program at the University of Nevada, Las Vegas. She spent eighteen months in Greece from June 2005–January 2006, on a sabbatical leave from UNLV and as a Senior Fulbright Scholar. Her project was to write a sequence of poems, "Eva's Voice," in the voice of an imaginary poet, Eva Victoria Perera, a Sephardic Jew from Thessaloniki, who survives the Holocaust. She has recorded a collaborative CD, *Wild Wind*, with musician, Frank Haney. She is serving as a consultant for Dr. Norris J. Chumley, Ph.D, on his new autobiographical documentary film and book, set in Bloomington, which deals with some of the racial issues portrayed in "Days of 1964 in Bloomington, Indiana." Her current writing project is tentatively entitled *Whence Our Names*, and explores the history of race and immigration in America.

She is Professor of English and Creative Writing Program at the University of Missouri, Columbia. With Scott Cairns, she is co-founder and co-director of the MU Summer Seminars in Greece, which as of 2011 is partnered with Cave Canem.

She lives and gardens in Columbia, Missouri with her daughter, Zoë, her husband, Craig Cones, three dogs, and two cats. She has traveled abroad in Greece, Spain, Italy, Turkey, China, Tibet, Burma, Nepal, Canada, Mexico, Guatemala, England, Holland, and elsewhere. She makes visual art, whenever and wherever she can.

Acknowledgments (continued from copyright page)

The Southern Review: "Her Scarlet Letters," "Back East Out West with Roger Williams,"
"My Friend Steve Asks if I Believe in the Afterlife,"
Slate: "Anger,"
Virginia Quarterly Review: "Children's Literature."

"Making Love After Catastrophe" appeared as "Making Love After September 11, 2001" in *September 11, 2001: American Writers Respond*, edited by William Heyen (Silver Spring, MD: Etruscan Press, 2002) and in *Literature: Reading Fiction, Poetry, & Drama*, Compact Edition, 2nd Edition, edited by Robert DiYanni (McGraw-Hill, 2003).

"First Amendment" appeared in *Red, White, and Blues: Poetic Vistas on the Promise of America*, edited by Virgil Suárez and Ryan Van Cleave (Iowa City, IA: University of Iowa Press, 2004).

For their help with these poems, I am grateful to my attentive readers: Tony Barnstone, Willis Barnstone, Tim Fuller, Cynthia Hogue, Khaled Mattawa, Alan Michael Parker, Lisa Rhoades, Mark Turpin, and Michael White. I thank my colleagues at the University of Nevada, Las Vegas for their moral support, especially Evelyn Gajowski, Chris Hudgins, Claudia Keelan, Doug Unger, and Richard Wiley. Doug and Richard—you are visionaries for launching the International Creative Writing Program at UNLV, which requires that students spend six weeks abroad and do a literary translation, the only program that is partnered with the Peace Corps. It was an honor and a delight to be a part of developing and growing the program I can't stop calling "ours." For sleepovers, dinners, spiritual sustenance, and lively, provocative, and inspiring discussion, I thank my fellow Las Vegas poets, Claudia Keelan and Donald Revell. For our many collaborations, for being partners in building and sustaining the Las Vegas literary community, I thank my colleagues at the College of Southern Nevada, especially Tina Eliopulos, Rich Logsdon, and Todd Moffett, who publish *Red Rock Review*, write grants, and sponsor wonderful readers and lecturers, . Thank you to the Las Vegas Poets Organization for the infrastructure that keeps the poetry flowing, watering the grounds of our beloved Mojave. Lenadams Dorris—the Enigma Café was a beautiful poetry sanctuary that lives on as our Eden. At the Enigma, I met my dear friends Gregory Crosby, Dayvid Jann Figler, Bruce Isaacson, and Todd Jones, navigational mates on the journey. I thank Lillie Englund for her friendship, for hosting readings at Imprints Day School, and for giving me the opportunity to teach poetry to kids, kindergarten through fifth grade. For their love and work, I thank my wonderful students, with whom I wrote the first drafts of many of these poems, playing the poetry game.

Finally, I honor the memory of Cliff Becker, Literature Director of the National Endowment for the Arts, whose friendship kept me going, in good cheer, until his death, May 17, 2005. His vision for art, especially the art of translation, continues to guide me in work and in spirit.